MINDFUL MENTALITY

TOLERANCE

BY VERONICA B. WILKINS

BLUE OWL BOOKS

TIPS FOR CAREGIVERS

Social and emotional learning (SEL) helps children connect with their emotions and gain a better understanding of themselves. Mindfulness can support this learning and help them develop a kind and inclusive mentality. By incorporating mindfulness and SEL into early learning, students can establish this mentality early and be better equipped to build strong connections and communities.

BEFORE READING

Talk to the reader about tolerance.

Discuss: What does tolerance mean to you? How do you show it? How do others show it to you?

AFTER READING

Talk to the reader about what he or she learned about tolerance from this book.

Discuss: What are some other ways you can show tolerance? Has there been a time when someone didn't tolerate or accept you? How did that feel?

SEL GOAL

Tolerance and empathy are key parts of social awareness. Students are aware of differences amongst themselves but may have a hard time tolerating and accepting them. Divide students into pairs and ask them to talk about things that make them similar and different. Change pairs and discuss again. Lead a group discussion about differences and similarities. Encourage learning about the differences in the group.

TABLE OF CONTENTS

CHAPTER 1

WHAT IS TOLERANCE?

Will is invited to his friend's house for dinner. But when they sit down to eat, he doesn't recognize the food on his plate. He is nervous to eat it.

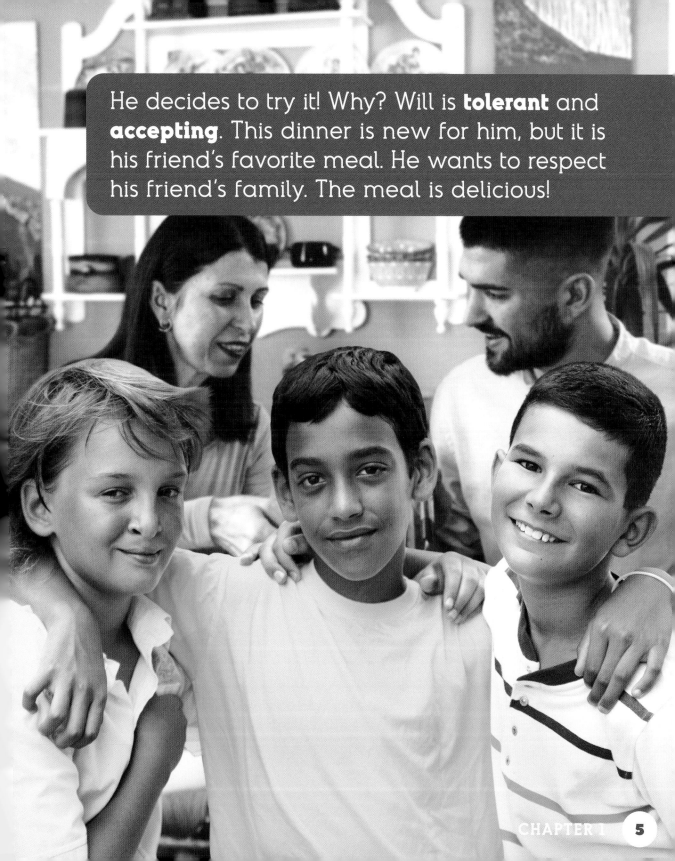

He decides to try it! Why? Will is **tolerant** and **accepting**. This dinner is new for him, but it is his friend's favorite meal. He wants to respect his friend's family. The meal is delicious!

Being tolerant is understanding that everyone is different. No one is better than someone else. Tolerance is accepting others as they are. You treat others how you would want to be treated. When you disagree, you work together to find a **compromise**.

Our **communities** are full of many different people. We learn from people who are different from us! When we are tolerant of differences, we build stronger, happier communities.

BE DIFFERENT!

Be proud of your differences! Sometimes, feeling different can feel uncomfortable. But differences make you unique. And they make life more interesting! What would it be like if we were all the same?

CHAPTER 2

SHOWING TOLERANCE

Leo has **autism**. He has a hard time speaking. Polly loves playing with him, but sometimes he is hard to understand. She is **patient**. She listens closely and waits to speak until Leo has finished telling his story.

hijab

Zora wears a hijab. Emma doesn't understand why, but she is polite. She uses kind words to ask Zora about it. She learns a lot! Zora's hijab is important to her. Her sisters and mother wear them, too!

Abby celebrates Hanukkah. Tilly celebrates Christmas. Tilly thinks Christmas is better. She talks to Abby about Hanukkah. She reads about it, too. After learning more about Abby's **culture**, she decides neither is better than the other. They are just different! She finds things she likes about both.

It is family day in Kenan's class. Both of his moms come. Teo brings his grandma. Sasha brings her mom and dad. Kelly brings her mom and older sister. Everyone's family looks different. But they are all there for the same reason. They all talk and play games together. Tolerance is seeing the ways in which we are similar.

Sani just moved to Paul's neighborhood. She is from another country. She doesn't speak English. Some kids don't want to play with her. But Paul's family just moved here last year. He remembers how it felt. He puts himself in Sani's shoes. He invites her to play. He shows **empathy**.

KNOW YOURSELF

Mindfulness can help us better understand our thoughts and feelings. This helps us better understand others, too. Think of a time when someone showed you tolerance. How did you feel? How do you think that person felt?

CHAPTER 3

HELP OTHERS SHOW TOLERANCE

When Jim joins ballet class, Beth teases him. She says ballet is just for girls. Sarah stands up for Jim. Boys and girls can all do the same things! Part of being tolerant is speaking up against **intolerance**.

Blake has been **bullying** Mel. Mike wants to help. He tells Blake to stop. When he doesn't, Mike gets the teacher. In doing this, he is a **role model** for tolerance.

How can you be more tolerant? Make friends with people who are different than you. Learn about other cultures. Share what you learn with your friends and classmates!

When we are tolerant, we show others we accept them. We make everyone feel like they belong. We make our communities stronger!

STRONG SELF-ESTEEM

Having good **self-esteem** can help you be tolerant. How? If you have good self-esteem, you won't feel the need to put others down. Build your self-esteem with mindfulness. Be aware of your thoughts. Think good things about yourself!

GOALS AND TOOLS

GROW WITH GOALS

Tolerance can be difficult, but you can get better with practice!

Goal: Sit with new peers at lunch. Ask them about themselves. See if you can find ways in which you are both different and similar. Learn more about your differences.

Goal: Learn about a holiday you do not celebrate. Research it online or in your school library. Write down things about that holiday you didn't know before and share them with your family and friends.

Goal: Learn to say hello in a different language! Practice saying it to new people you meet.

MINDFULNESS EXERCISE

Understanding your own emotions can help you understand the emotions of others. Try this activity to better identify and understand emotions.

1. Close your eyes. Take deep breaths. Reflect on your day.

2. Make a list of the emotions that you felt today.

3. When else have you felt these emotions? Have you noticed these emotions in others? When?

4. How do you react when you feel these emotions? How can you respond to others when they experience these emotions?

GLOSSARY

accepting
Agreeing that something is correct, satisfactory, or enough.

autism
A condition that causes someone to have trouble learning, communicating, and forming relationships with people.

bullying
Frightening or picking on people with repeated aggressive behavior.

communities
Groups of people who have something in common.

compromise
An agreement that is reached after people with opposing views each give up some of their demands.

culture
The ideas, customs, traditions, and way of life of a group of people.

empathy
The ability to understand and be sensitive to the thoughts and feelings of others.

intolerance
The inability or unwillingness to accept another kind of person, idea, or behavior.

mindfulness
A mentality achieved by focusing on the present moment and calmly recognizing and accepting your feelings, thoughts, and sensations.

patient
Able to put up with problems or delays without getting angry or upset.

role model
Someone whose behavior in a certain area is imitated by others.

self-esteem
A feeling of personal pride and respect for yourself.

tolerant
Willing to respect and accept the customs, beliefs, and opinions of others.

TO LEARN MORE

Finding more information is as easy as 1, 2, 3.

1. Go to www.factsurfer.com

2. Enter "**tolerance**" into the search box.

3. Choose your cover to see a list of websites.

INDEX

Blue Owl Books are published by Jump!, 5357 Penn Avenue South, Minneapolis, MN 55419, www.jumplibrary.com

Library of Congress Cataloging-in-Publication Data

Names: Wilkins, Veronica B., 1994– author.
Title: Tolerance / Veronica B. Wilkins.
Description: Minneapolis: Jump!, Inc., 2021. | Series: Mindful mentality | Includes index.
Audience: Ages 7–10 | Audience: Grades 2–3
Identifiers: LCCN 2020002920 (print)
LCCN 2020002921 (ebook)
ISBN 9781645273929 (hardcover)
ISBN 9781645273936 (paperback)
ISBN 9781645273943 (ebook)
Subjects: LCSH: Toleration–Juvenile literature. | Mindfulness (Psychology)–Juvenile literature.
Classification: LCC HM1271 .W55 2021 (print)
LCC HM1271 (ebook) | DDC 179/.9–dc23
LC record available at https://lccn.loc.gov/2020002920
LC ebook record available at https://lccn.loc.gov/2020002921

Editor: Jenna Gleisner
Designer: Molly Ballanger

Photo Credits: FatCamera/iStock, cover, 11; JBryson/iStock, 1; michaeljung/Shutterstock, 3, 10 (right); bonchan/Shutterstock, 4; LaraP_photo/Shutterstock, 5 (foreground); Dejan Dundjerski/Shutterstock, 5 (background); monkeybusinessimages/iStock, 6–7, 19 (background); Jose Luis Pelaez Inc/Getty, 8–9; AnnGaysorn/Shutterstock, 10 (left); pushlama/iStock, 12–13; visualspace/iStock, 14–15; Robert Kneschke/Shutterstock, 16–17; Sean Nel/Shutterstock, 18; Asier Romero/Shutterstock, 19 (boy); shironosov/iStock, 19 (girl); kali9/iStock, 20–21.

Printed in the United States of America at Corporate Graphics in North Mankato, Minnesota.